T

Endangered
FOREST ANIMALS

Marie Allgor

PowerKiDS press.

New York

Published in 2013 by The Rosen Publishing Group, Inc.
29 East 21st Street, New York, NY 10010

First Edition

Editor: Jennifer Way
Book Design: Julio Gil

Photo Credits: Cover Kristof Degreef/Shutterstock.com; pp. 4, 11 RFCD GeoAtlas; p. 5 Natalia Bratslavsky/Shutterstock.com; p. 5 (inset) Julian W/Shutterstock.com; p. 6–7 Pecold/Shutterstock.com; p. 7 (inset) TTphoto/Shutterstock.com; p. 9 Top Photo Group/Thinkstock; p. 10 Hemera/Thinkstock; p. 11 iStockphoto/Thinkstock; p. 12 Michael Hall/Photonica/Getty Images; pp. 13, 17 Stanley Breeden/National Geographic/Getty Images; p. 14 Hugh Lansdown/Shutterstock.com; p. 15 (main) John Mitchell/Oxford Scientific/Getty Images; p. 15 Lenice Harris/Shutterstock.com; p. 18 Norman Chan/Shutterstock.com; p. 19 (main) Hung Chung Chih/Shutterstock.com; p. 19 Ryan Morgan/Shutterstock.com; p. 20 © Anderson, Vickie/Animals Animals - Earth Scenes; p. 21 John L. Absher/Shutterstock.com; p. 22 Mikhail Olykainen/Shutterstock.com.

Library of Congress Cataloging-in-Publication Data

Allgor, Marie.
  Endangered forest animals / by Marie Allgor. — 1st ed.
      p. cm. — (Save Earth's animals!)
  Includes index.
  ISBN 978-1-4488-7424-8 (library binding) — ISBN 978-1-4488-7497-2 (pbk.) — ISBN 978-1-4488-7571-9 (6-pack)
  1. Endangered species—Juvenile literature. 2. Forest animals—Juvenile literature. 3. Forest ecology—Juvenile literature. 4. Wildlife conservation—Juvenile literature. I. Title.
  QL83.A4385 2013
  591.68—dc23

                         2011052946

Manufactured in China

CPSIA Compliance Information: Batch # WKTS12PK: For Further Information contact Rosen Publishing, New York, New York at 1-800-237-9932

Contents

Welcome to the Forest!

When we think of forests, we think of trees. Trees are part of what defines the world's forests. There are forests where **deciduous**, or leafy, trees grow. There are also forests where **coniferous**, or evergreen, trees grow.

This map shows where forest biomes are found.

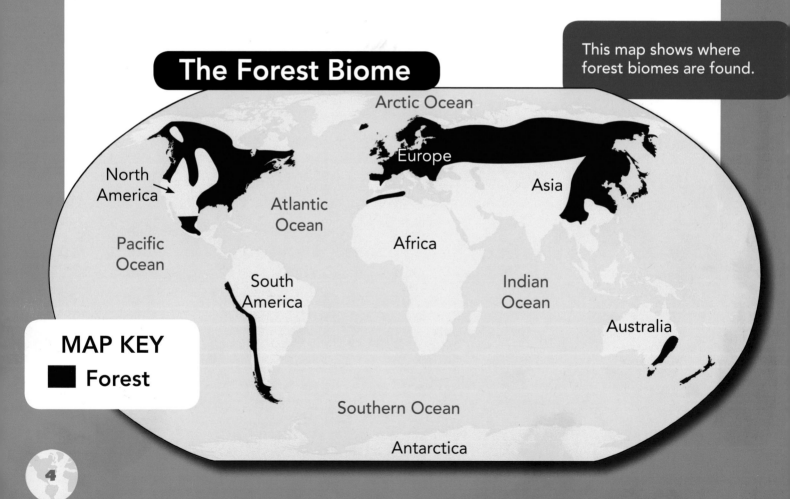

The Forest Biome

Arctic Ocean

Europe

Asia

North America

Atlantic Ocean

Pacific Ocean

Africa

South America

Indian Ocean

Australia

MAP KEY

■ Forest

Southern Ocean

Antarctica

This elk is grazing in a forest full of coniferous trees in Washington.

The numbat is an endangered animal that lives in deciduous forests in Australia.

Forests are important. They provide homes for countless animals. They help keep the air healthy. Many of the world's forests are in trouble because of things such as trees being cut down or wildfires. When a forest is in trouble, this means the animals that live there are in trouble, too. This book will introduce you to some of the world's **endangered** forest animals.

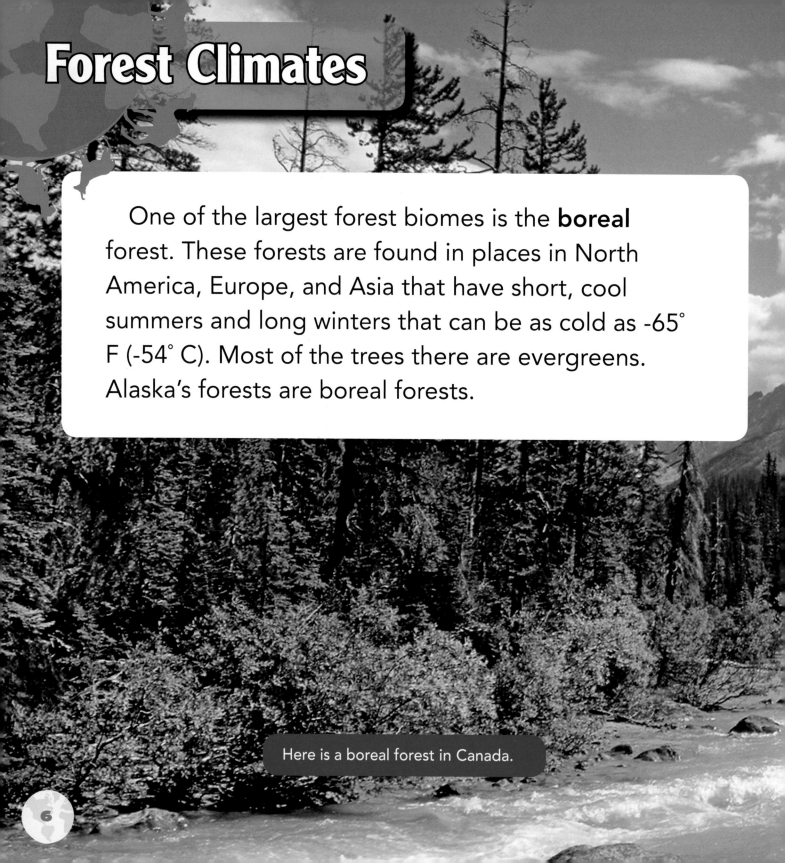

Forest Climates

One of the largest forest biomes is the **boreal** forest. These forests are found in places in North America, Europe, and Asia that have short, cool summers and long winters that can be as cold as -65° F (-54° C). Most of the trees there are evergreens. Alaska's forests are boreal forests.

Here is a boreal forest in Canada.

Woodpeckers, like the one shown here, make their homes in both temperate and boreal forests.

Temperate forests have milder, shorter winters than boreal forests. There are leafy trees that drop their leaves in autumn, such as oaks, maples, and elms, there. These forests are found in North America, South America, Europe, and Asia. In mixed forests, there are both evergreens and leafy trees.

Habitats in the Forest

Plenty of animals make their homes in Earth's forests. In boreal forests, there are deer, wolves, and small **mammals**. Many of the mammals in boreal forests live in dens or burrows and may **hibernate** during the long, cold winters. Groundhogs are animals that hibernate in the winter. Bears sleep through much of the winter, but they are not true hibernators.

Birds make their nests in tree branches in both temperate and boreal forests.

Temperate deciduous forests have more different kinds of wildlife in them because the climate is good for a wider variety of mammals and birds, such as robins. Reptiles and other cold-blooded animals might live in temperate forests, too.

The Forest's Endangered Animals

Forests take up about one-third of Earth's land. People are cutting a huge number of trees each year for lumber or to make way for farms, roads, homes, and businesses. The animals on these pages are endangered mainly due to these human activities.

MAP KEY

Red Panda
Leadbeater's Possum
Corroboree Frog
Idaho Ground Squirrel
Dhole

Dhole

1. Leadbeater's Possum

There are fewer than 2,500 Leadbeater's possums left in the world. Scientists expect this number to drop by 90 percent over the next 30 years.

2. Dhole

There are fewer than 2,500 dholes, a kind of wild dog, living in the forests of Asia today. There are about 112 dholes living in zoos around the world.

Where Forest Animals Live

Arctic Ocean

Area of Detail

Montana

North America

Europe

Atlantic Ocean

Asia

Oregon Idaho

Africa

Pacific Ocean

South America

Indian Ocean

Australia

Area of Detail

New South Wales

Victoria

Southern Ocean

Antarctica

3. Corroboree Frog

The corroboree frog is listed as **critically** endangered because its numbers have dropped by more than 80 percent in the past 10 years.

Red Panda

4. Red Panda

The red panda lives in forests in Bhutan, China, India, Myanmar, and Nepal. There are fewer than 10,000 of these animals left in the wild, and their numbers are continuing to drop. That is why the red panda is listed as **vulnerable**.

5. Idaho Ground Squirrel

One of the dangers to the Idaho ground squirrel comes from introduced grass **species** that are crowding out the grasses these squirrels commonly eat.

Leadbeater's Possum

The Leadbeater's possum lives in a small part of Victoria, Australia. This **nocturnal** animal needs forests with lots of old, hollow trees. It uses these trees to hide, sleep, and build nests for its young.

Sadly, Leadbeater's possums' habitat is in danger. The trees where these possums make their homes

In 2009, wildfires burned more than 1.1 million acres (450,000 ha) of land in Victoria, Australia. This area includes the Leadbeater's possum's habitat.

The tail of the Leadbeater's possum helps it keep its balance as it moves through trees.

are rotting and falling down. There are not enough younger trees with hollows to give these animals the shelter they need. The forests where the Leadbeater's possum lives are also being hurt by wildfires, logging, and climate change. Scientists think this species will be extinct in about 30 years.

Dhole

Dholes are a species of wild dog that lives in many kinds of forest habitats in Asia. Dholes live together in large groups, called clans. They generally break into smaller packs to hunt. They eat large animals such as deer, wild boars, and water buffalo.

Dholes hunt wild water buffalo, shown here. These animals are found in open, grassy areas near swamps and rivers.

Dholes look like dogs, but they are more closely related to jackals than they are to wolves or domestic dogs.

Wild boars are close relatives of domestic pigs. Today they are found in Asia, Europe, and parts of Africa.

These hunters once padded through forests throughout much of Asia. Today they are much harder to find. This is because much of their habitat is being taken over for human use. As the forests where they live get smaller, so do the number of **prey** that live there. With less to eat, dholes often get sick and die.

Corroboree Frog

The corroboree frog is a beautiful frog with striking black and yellow markings. It lives in forests as well as in grasslands in Australia's Snowy Mountains.

There are two species of corroboree frogs. They are the northern corroboree frog and the southern corroboree frog. Both species are endangered.

Scientists think there are only about 250 of these frogs still living in the wild. No one is quite sure why this frog is in so much trouble. Its numbers may be dropping due to illness or the introduction of tree species that have changed its habitat. There have also been wildfires that destroyed most of these frogs' habitat. In another 10 years, all of these frogs could be gone from the wild.

Red Panda

When you think of pandas, you likely picture the black-and-white giant panda. Red pandas do not look much like these better-known pandas. These two animals do share one common feature, though. They both eat bamboo and lots of it!

The red panda's body is about the size of a large cat's. The red panda's tail is about as long as its body.

The habitat of the giant panda, shown here, overlaps with that of the red panda.

This red panda is eating bamboo. Red pandas also eat fruits, eggs, and plant roots.

The biggest problems facing the red panda are habitat loss and poaching. Poaching is illegal hunting. As a species, the red panda is listed as vulnerable. In some parts of its range, such as Nepal, the red panda is nearly extinct. Laws are in place to help protect the red panda. Hopefully, these measures will keep its numbers from dropping further.

Idaho Ground Squirrel

The squirrels you see in parks are part of a large family of animals that includes chipmunks, prairie dogs, tree squirrels, and ground squirrels. Some members of this family are in trouble. The Idaho ground squirrel is an endangered squirrel that lives at the edges of forests of ponderosa pines and Douglas firs in that state.

This squirrel has become endangered largely due to habitat loss. This can lead to fragmentation,

The Idaho ground squirrel, shown here, looks for food in the meadows near its forest home.

The red-tailed hawk, shown here, is a predator of small animals such as the Idaho ground squirrel.

or the habitat getting broken up into small, unconnected areas. Scientists think there are at least a few thousand of these squirrels left, but the numbers are going down.

Save Forest Animals!

Forest habitats are rich and full of life. When we cut down forests and do not replace the trees, it hurts the plants and animals there.

In some places, trees are cut down faster than new trees can grow to replace them. This is called deforestation.

Many species have already become extinct, and others are endangered. When plants and animals become extinct due to human actions, this hurts our planet. Groups such as the World Wildlife Fund work to protect endangered animals. They also give people information about how to get involved in helping endangered animals.

Glossary

BOREAL (BOR-ee-ul) Having to do with northern places with lots of coniferous forests.

CONIFEROUS (kah-NIH-fur-us) Having cones and needlelike leaves.

CRITICALLY (KRIH-tih-kuh-lee) Being at a turning point.

DECIDUOUS (deh-SIH-joo-us) Having leaves that fall off every year.

ENDANGERED (in-DAYN-jerd) In danger of no longer existing.

HIBERNATE (HY-bur-nayt) To spend the winter in a sleeplike state.

MAMMALS (MA-mulz) Warm-blooded animals that have backbones and hair, breathe air, and feed milk to their young.

NOCTURNAL (nok-TUR-nul) Active during the night.

PREY (PRAY) An animal that is hunted by another animal for food.

SPECIES (SPEE-sheez) One kind of living thing. All people are one species.

TEMPERATE (TEM-puh-rut) Not too hot or too cold.

VULNERABLE (VUL-neh-ruh-bel) Open to being hurt or becoming extinct.

Index

Websites

Due to the changing nature of Internet links, PowerKids Press has developed an online list of websites related to the subject of this book. This site is updated regularly. Please use this link to access the list: www.powerkidslinks.com/sea/forest/